Pooh's Yummy Cookbook

Bath · New York · Singapore · Hong Kong · Cologne · Delhi
Melbourne · Amsterdam · Johannesburg · Auckland · Shenzhen

First edition published by Parragon in 2011

Parragon
Queen Street House
4 Queen Street
Bath BA1 1HE, UK

ISBN 9 78-1-4454-2901-4

Printed in China

This book belongs to

_____

_____

Instructions

Baking is so much fun, so get ready for some recipe magic!

All these yummy recipes have been created for you to cook with the help of Mom, Dad, or another grown-up. Always make sure they are with you when you start each recipe—they are there to help their favorite friend—you!

Before you can start cooking, there is some preparation to do! So put on your handy apron, wash your hands and check the next page to make sure you have everything you need.

You will need

Here are some things you will need— get them out in advance, so they are on hand!

- A large mixing bowl
- A wooden spoon
- A sifter
- A tablespoon
- Some baking trays
- Some cozy oven mitts!

Early one morning...

...Winnie the Pooh decided it was the perfect day for some cooking and baking! Before you head to the kitchen with Pooh and his friends, use the lines below to record your very own splendid ideas.

My favorite food is

_____

_____

A new ingredient I am going to try is

_____

_____

My favorite drink is

_____

_____

One thing I am looking forward to making is

_____

_____

Who is going to help me with my recipes?

_____

_____

All the friends in the Hundred-Acre Wood love to bake for those that are most special to them.

Name _____

What I will bake for them

_____

Name _____

What I will bake for them

_____

Name _____

What I will bake for them

_____

Name _____

What I will bake for them

_____

Name _____

What I will bake for them

_____

Use the spaces to decide who will taste your treats!

Hunny Cake

Ingredients:

- 3 eggs
- 3oz sugar
- 3½oz self-rising flour

- 2 tablespoons of honey
- 1 pinch of salt

 Indicates parental supervision required.

1. Separate the egg yolks from the whites, and place into two separate bowls.
2. Add sugar and honey to the yolks, and beat well.
3. Mix in spoonfuls of flour.
4. Add a pinch of salt to the egg whites, and whisk until stiff.
5. Gently mix the egg whites into the yolk mixture.

Hunny

6. Pour into a round buttered cake tin. Cook for 30 minutes at 360°f.

7. Remove from the oven and allow to cool.

8. Get a grown-up to cut the cake in half, spread with jelly and cream, and sandwich together.

If you wish, decorate the top of your cake with frosting. Enjoy with your friends!

How did you do?

Use this space to tell us how well you did, and keep it for the next time you try the recipe!

My hunny cake was:

_____

The best thing about this recipe was:

_____

The hardest thing about this recipe was:

_____

One thing I would do differently next time is:

_____

Who helped me with this recipe?:

_____

A Comforting Sort of Thing

The best thing about cooking and baking is sharing the treats with all your friends. Once everyone has tried your recipe, fill in this page.

Who tried my hunny cake

_____

What they thought

_____

Who tried my hunny cake

_____

What they thought

_____

Who tried my hunny cake

_____

What they thought

_____

Who tried my hunny cake

_____

What they thought

_____

_____

Hint: Next time you try this recipe, read what everyone thought so you can make the cake even tastier!

A Honey of a Day

It was a sunny day in the Hundred-Acre Wood, and Pooh—as Pooh often does—had honey on his mind. "Today is a honey of a day," he said to himself. Pooh decided he needed to have a good think about his honey meal, so he headed to his Thoughtful Spot.

"Think, think, think," Pooh mumbled to himself. But nothing came to mind. Luckily, Piglet soon arrived with a very good idea. "For small animals like me, small honey cakes are the perfect treat."

Suddenly, a big, bouncy creature bounded over and knocked Pooh flat on his back. It was Tigger! "Tiggers don't like honey!" he said. "What you should bake is a tigger cake, with scrumdelicious stripes of jelly. Yummy!"

Before long, Owl and Rabbit arrived. Owl explained that the most sensible thing to do was to make honey sandwiches for the friends to share while he told one of his stories.

Rabbit suggested that Pooh use some vegetables from his garden to bake a honey and vegetable pie—but Pooh didn't like the sound of that.

Pooh decided that asking his rumbly tummy was the best idea. The loudest rumblings rumbled at the thought of Piglet's honey cakes, so that was what Pooh baked on that honey of a day in the Hundred-Acre Wood.

A Snack for Pooh!

All Pooh's friends gave him lots of yummy ideas for snacks—even if his rumbly tummy had the best idea of all!

Think about who you would like to make a snack for. What's their favorite food? What ingredients would they like the most? Maybe they like to munch on carrot sticks like Rabbit, or do they prefer sweet things, like Pooh?

Once you have decided, use the page opposite to create your very own recipe, using the hints as you go along.

Now it's your turn! Use the box below to create your ideal Hundred-Acre Wood snack recipe.

What is your recipe called?

_____

Who are you making it for?

_____

What are the ingredients?

_____

_____

_____

How will you do it?

_____

_____

_____

Fruit 'n' Nut Cookies

Ingredients (makes 10 cookies):

- 3oz raisins
- 3½oz plain flour
- 2oz rolled oats
- 1¾oz walnuts
- 4½oz unsalted butter cut into small pieces
- 2½oz light brown sugar
- 2 tbsp honey

Equipment:

- scissors
- large mixing bowl
- wooden spoon
- small saucepan
- tablespoon
- 2 baking sheets lightly greased
- wire cooling rack

Indicates parental supervision required.

1 Preheat the oven to 350°F.

2 Put the raisins in a large bowl with the flour, oats, and walnuts. Using a wooden spoon, stir until mixed together.

3 Put the butter, brown sugar and honey in a saucepan and heat gently, stirring from time to time, until melted.

4 👫 Pour the butter mixture into the bowl and stir to make a soft, chunky dough.

5 Place heaped tablespoons of the dough onto the baking sheets and flatten the tops a little—the cookies should be about 1 inch wide and 1/2 inch thick. Make sure you leave space between the cookies so they can spread.

6 👫 Bake for 15 minutes, until golden brown. Remove from the oven and leave the cookies to cool a for a few minutes, then move to a wire rack to cool and become crisp.

How did you do?

Use this space to tell us how well you did, and keep it for the next time you try the recipe!

My cookies were:

The best thing about this recipe was:

The hardest thing about this recipe was:

One thing I would do differently next time is:

Who helped me with this recipe?

A Happy Sort of Thing

The best thing about cooking and baking is sharing the treats with all your friends. Once everyone has tried your recipe, fill in this page.

Who tried my cookies
_____
What they thought
_____

Who tried my cookies
_____
What they thought
_____

Who tried my cookies
_____
What they thought
_____

Who tried my cookies
_____
What they thought
_____

Hint: Next time you try this recipe, read what everyone thought so you can make the cookies even tastier!

Cheer Up, Eeyore

It was a rainy day in the Hundred-Acre Wood, and Eeyore, the old gray donkey was sitting in his little house. "Drip, drip, drip" went the rain, right on to Eeyore's head.

Pooh and Piglet walked by, and noticed Eeyore looking gloomy. "Eeyore! Aren't you enjoying this rainy, splish-splashy sort of day?" Pooh asked. Eeyore gave a big sigh. "The rain is dripping on my head. My tail is wet. Seems like everyone has a reason to be cheerful except Eeyore."

Piglet tugged on Pooh's hand. "Pooh! I have an idea of something we could do to cheer up Eeyore! Come on!" Piglet and Pooh ran back to Piglet's house.

Later on Eeyore was still wet and gloomy.
Just then—SPLASH! Tigger landed in a
puddle right in front of him! "Hoo-hoo-hoo!
I hear there's some kind of splendiferous
surprise happening at Piglet's house.
Come on!"

When they arrived, a most delicious smell was floating
out of Piglet's house. They opened the door, and...

"Surprise! Eeyore, we are sorry your house is drippy, and damp.
We've made you your favorite cake to cheer you up." Pooh
and Piglet were standing next to a table, on which rested a
delicious-looking cake.

Eeyore smiled slowly. "Thanks Pooh. Thanks Piglet," he said,
and decided to share his cake with his best friends. All was
well in the Hundred-Acre Wood.

A Cake for Eeyore

Pooh and Piglet wanted to cheer up their friend Eeyore, so they baked him a delicious cake as a surprise.

Think about who you would like to bake a cake for. Does anyone need cheering up? Or maybe someone has done something nice for you, and you would like to thank them?

What kind of cake will you make—maybe a chocolate cake, or a strawberry shortcake? There's always Rabbit's favorite—carrot cake! There are lots to choose from! Once you have decided, use the page opposite to create your very own recipe, using the hints as you go along.

Hunny

Hunny

Now it's your turn! Use the box below to create your ideal Hundred-Acre Wood cake recipe.

What is your recipe called?

_____

Who are you making it for?

_____

What are the ingredients?

_____

_____

_____

How will you do it?

_____

_____

_____

Gingerbread Animals

Ingredients (makes approx. 10):

- 6oz plain flour, plus extra if needed
- 2 tsp ground ginger
- ½ tsp baking soda
- 2oz unsalted butter, cut into small pieces
- 3oz light brown sugar
- 2 tbsp honey
- 1 egg, lightly beaten
- tubes of writing icing in different colors, to decorate

👪 Indicates parental supervision required.

1 Sift the flour, ginger, and baking soda into a large bowl. Rub in the butter using your fingertips until the mixture looks like fine breadcrumbs.

2 👪 Gently heat the brown sugar and honey in a saucepan until melted. Pour into the bowl, then add the egg.

3 👪 Mix with a wooden spoon to make a soft dough. If it is too sticky, add a little more flour and mix again. Wrap in plastic wrap and chill for 30 minutes. Preheat the oven at 375°F.

4 Lightly flour the work surface and rolling pin, then unwrap the dough and roll out until it is about 1 inch thick. Use animal shaped cookie cutters to stamp out about 10 animal shapes, re-rolling the dough as necessary.

5 👪 Carefully place the cookies on the baking sheet and bake for 12-15 minutes, until just crisp. Remove from the oven and leave to cool a little.

6 Move the cookies to a wire rack. When cool, decorate with writing icing.

You don't always have to make gingerbread animals—you could make gingerbread flowers, or triangles! Use the space below to draw something new, and make it out of gingerbread next time.

What did they think?

It's time to see what others thought of your recipe!

Ask your friends to rank your cookies 1-5 stars for your recipe, and color in how many you got!

It's 1 star for 'try again' and 5 for 'that was delicious!'

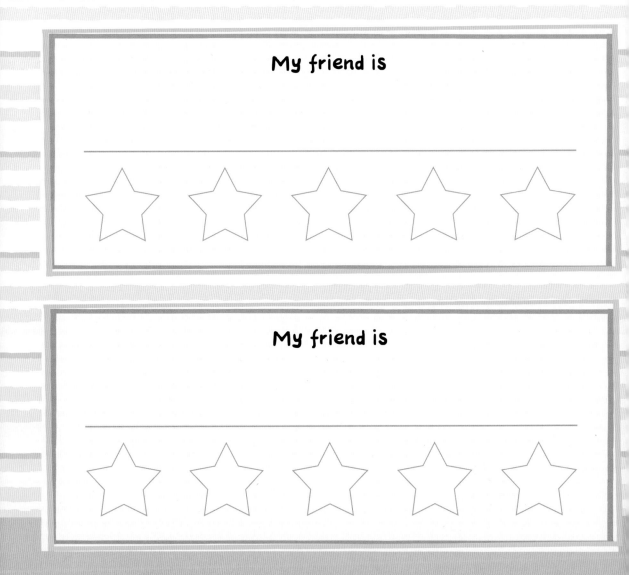

My friend is

_____

My friend is

_____

My friend is

_____

My friend is

_____

My friend is

_____

Banana Bread

Ingredients:

- 5 ripe, peeled bananas
- 7oz self-rising white flour
- 1½oz self-rising wholewheat flour
- 1 tsp baking powder
- 4½oz unsalted butter, cut into small pieces, chilled

- 3 large eggs, lightly beaten
- 3½oz superfine sugar
- 3½oz chopped dried fruit
- Powdered sugar, for dusting

Indicates parental supervision required.

Equipment:

- medium mixing bowl
- fork
- sifter
- large mixing bowl
- wooden spoon
- 900g (2lb) loaf pan, greased and lined
- wire cooling rack

1 Preheat the oven to 350°F. Break the bananas up into a medium bowl, then mash them with a fork until almost smooth.

2 Sift both types of flour and the baking powder into a large bowl then add the butter.

3 Using your fingertips, rub the butter into the flour mixture until it looks like fine breadcrumbs.

4 Stir in the eggs, superfine sugar, bananas, and dried fruit using a wooden spoon, then pour into the loaf pan.

5 Level the top using the back of the spoon, then bake for about 50-60 minutes, until risen and golden brown.

6 Remove from the oven and leave the cake to cool in the pan for 10 minutes, then flip onto a wire rack. Dust with powdered sugar before cutting.

How did you do?

My banana bread was:

_____

The best thing about this recipe was:

_____

The hardest thing about this recipe was:

_____

One thing I would do differently next time is:

_____

Who helped me with this recipe?

_____

Use this space to tell us how well you did, and keep it for the next time you try the recipe!

A Scrummy Sort of Thing

The best thing about cooking and baking is sharing the treats with all your friends. Once everyone has tried your recipe, fill in this page.

Who tried my banana bread

_____

What they thought

_____

Who tried my banana bread

_____

What they thought

_____

Who tried my banana bread

_____

What they thought

_____

Who tried my banana bread

_____

What they thought

_____

Hint: Next time you try this recipe, read what everyone thought so you can make the bread even tastier!

A Helping Hand

One day in the Hundred-Acre Wood, Pooh was having a problem. "Oh, bother." he said to himself. His favorite honeypot was broken! "Now what will I keep all my lovely honey in?"

Just then, Piglet knocked on his door.

"Oh, hello Piglet." Pooh said glumly. Piglet noticed the broken honeypot on the floor next to Pooh.

"Oh no P-P-Pooh!" Piglet said. He picked up the broken pieces and thought for a moment.

"I know!" cried Piglet. He ran all the way home, and all the way back. "Here!"

Pooh watched as Piglet used his special 'Fix-it' glue to stick the honeypot back together. It was as good as new!

Pooh was so happy Piglet helped him fix his honeypot! After Piglet had gone home, Pooh wanted to do something very special to thank him. He asked Kanga to help him make lots and lots of lovely little cookies, shaped like butterflies.

The next day, Pooh took the special cookies to Piglet's house.

"Thank you so much, Piglet," said Pooh, and the two friends hugged. Then Piglet shared his delicious butterfly cookies with his best friend.

Treats for Piglet!

Pooh wanted to make some tasty cookies for Piglet, because he had been so kind and helpful to him.

Think about who you would like to bake cookies for. Maybe a family member, or a best friend? You can even make them just for yourself!

Pooh used **honey** in his recipe because that's his favorite ingredient! What would you use in your recipe— maybe bananas? Raisins? Chocolate? There are lots of choices!

Once you have decided, use the page opposite to create your very own recipe, using the hints as you go along.

Now it's your turn. Use the box below
to create your ideal Hundred-Acre Wood cookie recipe.

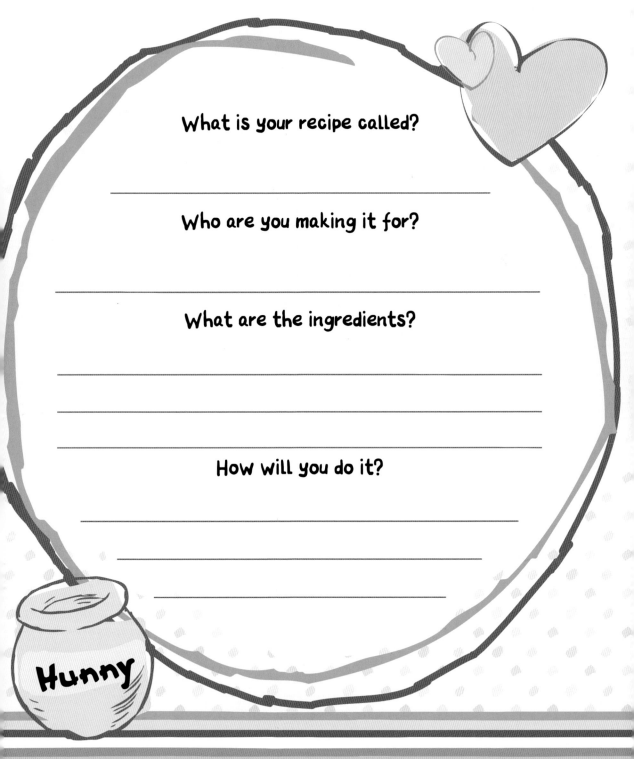

What is your recipe called?

_____

Who are you making it for?

_____

What are the ingredients?

_____

_____

_____

How will you do it?

_____

_____

_____

Hunny

Carrot Cake Squares

Ingredients (makes 16 squares):

- 3½oz wholewheat self-rising flour
- 5oz white self-rising flour
- 1 tsp baking powder
- 2 tsp ground allspice
- 8oz dark brown sugar
- 8oz carrots, peeled and grated
- 3 large eggs, lightly beaten
- 1 cup sunflower oil

Frosting:
- 5oz low-fat cream cheese
- 4 tbsp unsalted butter, softened
- 1 tsp vanilla extract
- 6oz powdered sugar
- yellow, red and green ready to roll icing, to decorate

Indicates parental supervision required.

1 Preheat the oven to 350°F. Sift both types of flour into a large bowl. Using a wooden spoon, stir in the baking powder, allspice, dark brown sugar, and carrots.

2 Add the eggs and oil, then stir until mixed together. Pour the mixture into the 10 inch square pan and smooth the top with the back of the spoon.

3 Bake for 50 minutes, until golden brown. Remove from the oven and leave to cool for 10 minutes, then place a wire rack on top and carefully flip the cake out.

4 When the cake is cool, beat the cream cheese, butter, vanilla extract, and powdered sugar in a medium bowl until smooth and creamy. Chill for 10 minutes.

5 Spread the frosting over the cake and smooth using a frosting spatula, then cut into 16 squares.

6 Mix together the yellow and red icing to make orange, then roll into 16 carrot shapes. Top each "carrot" with a small piece of green icing, then place 1 on top of each square.

How did you do?

Use this space to tell us how well you did, and keep it for the next time you try the recipe!

My carrot cakes were:

_____

The best thing about this recipe was:

_____

The hardest thing about this recipe was:

_____

One thing I would do differently next time is:

_____

Who helped me with this recipe?

_____

A Delicious Sort of Thing

The best thing about cooking and baking is sharing the treats with all your friends. Once everyone has tried your recipe, fill in this page.

Who tried my carrot cakes

_____

What they thought

_____

Who tried my carrot cakes

_____

What they thought

_____

Hint: Next time you try this recipe, read what everyone thought so you can make the cakes even tastier!

Who tried my carrot cakes

_____

What they thought

_____

Who tried my carrot cakes

_____

What they thought

_____

Fruit Smoothies

Ingredients (makes 1 smoothie):

Berry Smoothie
- 1 small banana
- 5oz fresh raspberries and strawberries
- 1.5 cups skim milk
- superfine sugar if required

Yogurt Smoothie
- 1 small banana
- 1 ripe pear
- 1 cup apple juice
- 1 cup yogurt
- 1 tsp vanilla extract
- 1 tbsp honey

Equipment:

- chopping board
- sharp knife
- teaspoon

- blender or food processor
- measuring cup

Indicates parental supervision required.

1. For the berry smoothie, slice the banana. Cut the strawberries in half if they are very large.

2. Place the fruit in the blender. Pour in the milk. Make sure the lid is on tight and blend until smooth.

3. Add sugar to taste. Pour into glasses and serve with straws.

1. For the yogurt smoothie, slice the banana. Peel, core, and chop the pear.

2. Place all the ingredients in the blender. Make sure the lid is on tight and blend until smooth.

3. Pour into glasses and serve.

For a change!
You can add crushed ice or ice cream to your smoothie to make a cooler drink for hot summer days.

How did you do?

Use this space to tell us how well you did, and keep it for the next time you try the recipe!

My smoothies were:

_____

The best thing about this recipe was:

_____

The hardest thing about this recipe was:

_____

One thing I would do differently next time is:

_____

Who helped me with this recipe?

_____

A Fruity Sort of Thing

The best thing about cooking and baking is sharing the treats with all your friends. Once everyone has tried your recipe, fill in this page.

Who tried my smoothies

_____

What they thought

_____

Who tried my smoothies

_____

What they thought

_____

Who tried my smoothies

_____

What they thought

_____

Who tried my smoothies

_____

What they thought

_____

_____

Hint: Next time you try this recipe, read what everyone thought so you can make the smoothies even tastier!

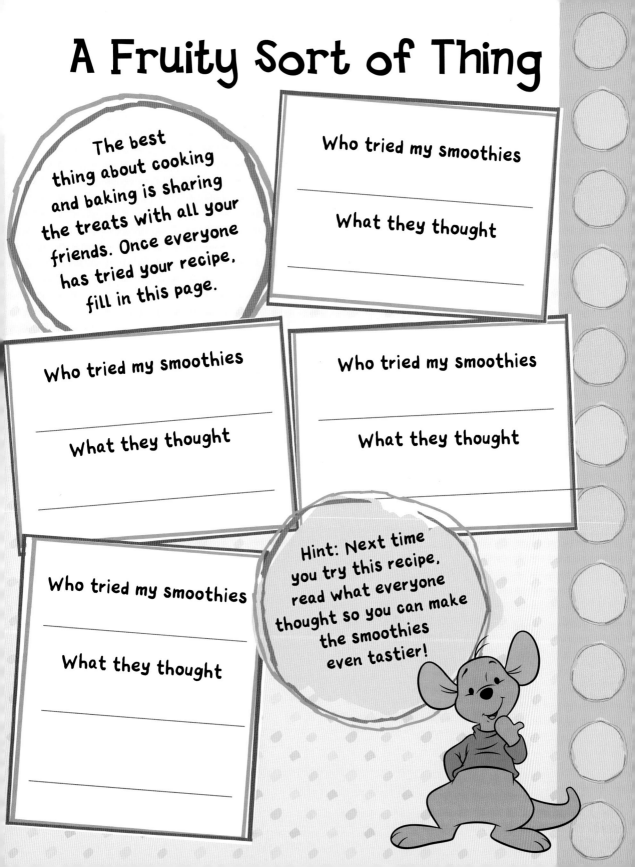

Decoration Time!

It's fun to use different shapes for cookies, candies, or even as icing on a cake! Trace over the pretty patterns below with tracing paper so you have a design for all kinds of friendly treats!

These button-shaped cookies can be threaded with colored ribbons to make pretty decorations. Use a toothpick to make 4 holes in each cookie before baking so it looks like a button. When cool, thread ribbon through the holes and tie into a bow.

It's time for some Hundred-Acre Wood ideas!

Think about what you have enjoyed the most, and use the lines below to write down some ideas to make even more new and exciting recipes!

My favorite recipe so far:

_____

What I could do to make it better:

_____

_____

_____

_____

Time to Decorate!

Oh no! Piglet has made a cake for the party tonight, but he hasn't had time to decorate it! Help him by drawing some pretty patterns on the top of the cake.

Perfect Crepes

Ingredients (makes approx. 6 crepes):

- 3½oz plain flour
- pinch of salt
- 1 egg, beaten
- 1½ cups milk

- 10 tsp butter or vegetable oil

To Serve:
- lemon juice
- superfine sugar

Equipment:

- sifter
- mixing bowl
- wooden spoon
- measuring cup
- 7 inch non-stick frying pan

- teaspoon
- plate
- wooden spatula
- parchment paper and tinfoil

Indicates parental supervision required.

1. Sift the flour and salt in the bowl. Make a 'well' in the center; add the egg and half the milk. Beat the egg and milk together.

2. Gradually mix in the flour. When the mixture is smooth with no lumps, beat in the rest of the milk. Carefully pour the mixture into the cup.

3. Heat the pan over a medium heat. Add a teaspoon of the butter or oil and swirl it around to cover the whole surface.

Serve them hot!

Serve the crepes while they are still hot. Sprinkle with sugar or drizzle with syrup and roll them up.

4. Pour in enough batter to cover the base. Swirl around the pan while tilting it so you have a thin, even layer. Cook for about 30 seconds.

5. Lift up the edge of the crepe to see if it is brown. Loosen round the edges and flip with the spatula. Cook the other side until golden brown.

6. Turn out each crepe onto a warm plate. Stack in layers with parchment paper. Cover with tinfoil and keep warm.

How did you do?

Use this space to tell us how well you did, and keep it for the next time you try the recipe!

My crepes were:

_____

The best thing about this recipe was:

_____

The hardest thing about this recipe was:

_____

One thing I would do differently next time is:

_____

Who helped me with this recipe?

_____

Perfect Crepes

The best thing about cooking and baking is sharing the treats with all your friends. Once everyone has tried your recipe, fill in this page.

Who tried my crepes
_____

What they thought
_____

Who tried my crepes
_____

What they thought
_____

Who tried my crepes
_____

What they thought
_____

Who tried my crepes
_____

What they thought
_____

Hint: Next time you try this recipe, read what everyone thought so you can make the crepes even tastier!

Rabbit's Picnic

It was a lovely afternoon in the Hundred-Acre Wood. Rabbit was humming happily as he prepared a delicious picnic for himself and his friends.

"Now," he said as he finished chopping carrots for himself, baking muffins for Pooh, and cooking the strawberry tarts for Piglet, "That seems to be everything!"

"Hello, Rabbit! I'm not too early am I?" Rabbit heard a little voice say. Piglet was at the door. "No, no, come in Piglet! Look at all the delicious treats I have prepared for everyone!" "It all looks yummy, Rabbit!" Piglet said, "but, um, what about Tigger?"

"Tigger!" Rabbit cried. "Piglet you're right —I have tarts for you, muffins for Pooh and cookies for Roo—but what do tiggers eat?"

Poor Rabbit looked very upset. There was hardly any time left to bake anything new! "Don't worry Rabbit—I'll help you!" said Piglet, and ran to the kitchen.

Later, Pooh, Owl, Eeyore, Kanga, Roo, and Tigger arrived at Rabbit's picnic, all spread out on a blanket in the sun.

"This looks splendiferous, Long Ears!" Tigger bounced up to the picnic. "Anything here for your favoritest, stripyiest friend?" Rabbit swallowed nervously. "Why, of course Tigger!" Rabbit held out a plate of sandwiches—and they were all shaped like little tiggers!

"Hoo-hoo-hoo! Tigger sandwiches! My favorite!" And Tigger ate every last one!

A Friendly Picnic

Rabbit planned a lovely picnic for everyone, with delicious treats they all loved—especially Tigger!

Think about something you might take to a picnic. You could make little sandwiches, and cut them into shapes? Or you could make cookies to share with everyone? Or maybe a delicious new drink for everyone to try.

Once you have decided, use the page opposite to create your very own recipe, using the hints as you go along.

Now it's your turn. Use the box below to create your ideal Hundred-Acre Wood picnic recipe.

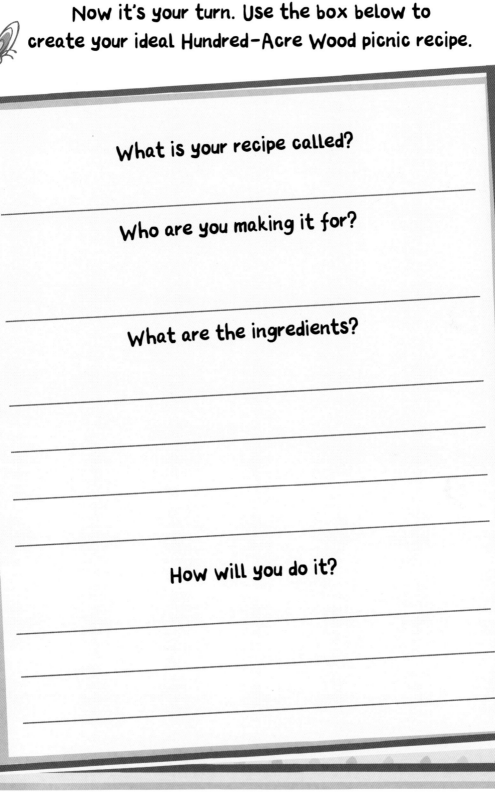

What is your recipe called?

_____

Who are you making it for?

_____

What are the ingredients?

_____

_____

_____

_____

How will you do it?

_____

_____

_____

Raisin Cookies

Ingredients (makes approx. 12):

- 3oz unsalted butter, cut into small pieces
- 10½oz self-rising flour
- 2½oz golden superfine sugar
- 2½oz raisins
- Half a cup of milk
- 1 large egg
- 1 tsp vanilla extract

Equipment:

- large mixing bowl
- wooden spoon
- measuring cup
- balloon whisk or fork
- tablespoon
- 2 baking trays, lined with parchment paper
- wire cooling rack

Indicates parental supervision required.

1 Preheat the oven to 375°F. In a large bowl, rub the butter into the flour with your fingertips until the mixture looks like fine breadcrumbs.

2 Stir in the superfine sugar, and raisins with a wooden spoon until evenly mixed.

3 Put the milk, egg, and vanilla extract in a cup and whisk together with a balloon whisk or fork.

4 Pour the mixture into the bowl and stir to make a chunky dough.

5 For each cookie, place 2 heaping tablespoons of the mixture on a baking tray. Repeat to make 12 cookies in total.

6 Bake for 15–18 minutes, until golden brown. Remove from the oven and leave the cookies to cool a little, then move to a wire rack.

How did you do?

Use this space to tell us how well you did, and keep it for the next time you try the recipe!

My raisin cookies were:

_____

The best thing about this recipe was:

_____

The hardest thing about this recipe was:

_____

One thing I would do differently next time is:

_____

Who helped me with this recipe?

_____

A Sharing Sort of Thing

The best thing about cooking and baking is sharing the treats with all your friends. Once everyone has tried your recipe, fill in this page.

Who tried my raisin cookies
_____

What they thought
_____

Who tried my raisin cookies
_____

What they thought
_____

Who tried my raisin cookies
_____

What they thought
_____

Who tried my raisin cookies
_____

What they thought
_____

Hint: Next time you try this recipe, read what everyone thought so you can make the raisin cookies even tastier!

Chocolate Brownies

Ingredients (makes 16 brownies):

- 4½oz unsalted butter, cut into small pieces
- 3½oz plain chocolate, broken into squares
- 2 large eggs
- 9¾oz dark brown superfine sugar
- 3oz plain flour
- 1 tsp baking powder
- 2 tbsp cocoa powder

Equipment:

- medium heatproof bowl
- medium saucepan
- wooden spoon
- large mixing bowl
- electric hand mixer
- sifter
- 10 inch square cake tin, greased and lined
- knife

1 Preheat the oven to 350°F. Put the butter and chocolate in a heatproof bowl placed over a saucepan containing 1 inch of water—make sure the bowl does not touch the water.

2 Bring the water to a simmer and melt the butter and chocolate, stirring once or twice. Carefully remove from the heat and leave to cool a little.

3 In a large mixing bowl, whisk the eggs and superfine sugar using an electric hand mixer for 5 minutes, until pale and fluffy. Stir in the melted chocolate mixture.

4 Sift the flour, baking powder and cocoa into the bowl and fold in until mixed together.

5 Pour into the cake pan and level the top using the back of the spoon.

6  Bake for 35–40 minutes, until it rises but is still a bit soft in the center. Remove from the oven and leave to cool in the tin a little, then turn out and cut into 16 squares.

Indicates parental supervision required.

How did you do?

Use this space to tell us how well you did, and keep it for the next time you try the recipe!

My brownies were:

_____

The best thing about this recipe was:

_____

The hardest thing about this recipe was:

_____

One thing I would do differently next time is:

_____

Who helped me with this recipe?

_____

A Yummy Sort of Thing

The best thing about cooking and baking is sharing the treats with all your friends. Once everyone has tried your recipe, fill in this page.

Who tried my brownies
_____
What they thought
_____

Who tried my brownies
_____
What they thought
_____

Hint: Next time you try this recipe, read what everyone thought so you can make the brownies even tastier!

Who tried my brownies
_____
What they thought
_____

Who tried my brownies
_____
What they thought
_____

Good Job!

It's time to see what others thought of your recipes!

Ask your friends to rank you from 1-5 stars for your recipes, and color in how many you got!

It's 1 star for 'try again' and 5 for 'that was yummy!'

My friend is

_____

☆ ☆ ☆ ☆ ☆

My friend is

_____

☆ ☆ ☆ ☆ ☆